RELIGIOUS LIBERTY AND STATE CONSTITUTIONS

RELIGIOUS LIBERTY AND STATE CONSTITUTIONS

☆ ☆ ☆ ☆ ☆ ☆ ☆ ☆ ☆ ☆ ☆

EDD DOERR & ALBERT J. MENENDEZ

Prometheus Books

59 John Glenn Drive
Buffalo, New York 14228-2197

Published 1993 by Prometheus Books

97 96 95 94 93   5 4 3 2 1

Library of Congress Cataloging-in-Publication Data

Doerr, Edd.
    Religious liberty and state constitutions / Edd Doerr and Albert J. Menendez.
    Includes bibliographical references.
    ISBN 0-87975-839-2
    1. Freedom of religion—United States—States. I. Menendez, Albert J.
II. Title.
KF4783.Z95D64   1993
342.73'0852—dc20
[347.302852]
                                                                    93-5867
                                                                       CIP

Published in cooperation with Americans for Religious Liberty, P.O. Box 6656, Silver Spring, Maryland 20916. Americans for Religious Liberty (ARL) is a nonprofit public interest educational organization, founded in 1981, dedicated to preserving the American tradition of religious, intellectual, and personal freedom in a pluralistic secular democratic state. Membership is open to all who share that purpose. ARL publishes a newsletter and other material, operates a speakers bureau, and has been involved in litigation in defense of separation of church and state and freedom of conscience. Inquiries are welcomed.

Printed in the United States of America on acid-free paper.

For Herenia and Shirley

Contents

8   Contents

Introduction

Between 1775 and 1791 Americans conceived, fought for, and established a new nation. This new nation, as Thomas Jefferson explained in the Declaration of Independence in 1776, was based on the proposition that all persons are created equal, that they have inherent natural rights ("Life, Liberty, and the Pursuit of Happiness"), that "to secure these rights, Governments are instituted among Men, deriving their just powers from the consent of the governed," and that "it is the Right of the People to alter or abolish" any form of government that does not secure the rights of the people.

In 1787, independence from Great Britain having been won by force of arms, representatives of the states met in Philadelphia to create a workable federal government, a limited government of delegated powers only, one which implemented, though imperfectly, the principles of the Declaration. The purposes of the new government, spelled out in the Preamble to the Constitution, were to be to "establish Justice, insure domestic Tranquillity, provide for the common defence, promote the general Welfare, and secure the Blessings of Liberty to ourselves and our Posterity."

Since the people of the United States had not only fought for six long years for political independence, but had also in the several states deliberately moved away from the European and

11

earlier colonial models of church-state union and religious intolerance, their representatives in Philadelphia carefully avoided granting the new government any power or authority whatever to meddle with or involve itself with religion. The Constitution they created limited the federal government to purely secular matters. Further, Article VI of the Constitution, in an important departure from colonial practice, stipulated that "no religious Test shall ever be required as a Qualification to any Office or public trust under the United States." The same article also prohibited mandatory oaths by providing that all members of the executive, legislative, and judicial branches "both of the United States and of the several states" may be bound by either an "Oath or *Affirmation*" (italics ours) to support the Constitution.

Thus the Constitution itself implied and implies the principle of separation of church and state, which the Constitution's principal architect, James Madison, and the Declaration's author, Thomas Jefferson, had championed and had seen enacted into law in Virginia only a short time before the Philadelphia convention. Indeed, Madison had spelled out the rationale for the separation principle in his 1785 Memorial and Remonstrance Against Religious Assessments, a short treatise aimed at securing passage of Jefferson's Bill for Establishing Religious Freedom in the Virginia legislature.

It might also be noted that the Constitution did not include even a perfunctory reference to a deity. Delegate Luther Martin of Maryland had proposed including a provision about belief in a Supreme Being, but, he wrote later, it was voted down. Martin opposed the Constitution for that reason.

Although the new Constitution represented the greatest single advance in the long evolution of democracy and freedom, it was viewed by many, including Jefferson, as containing a serious defect, the absence of an explicit bill of rights. Ratification of the new charter of government hinged on the promises of politicians to add a bill of rights to the Constitution as soon as possible, promises carried out by the first Congress, which in 1789 proposed amendments which were ratified by the states by the end of 1791.

The First Amendment provides that, "Congress shall make no law respecting an establishment of religion, or prohibiting the free exercise thereof; . . ."

President Jefferson, writing to the Danbury Baptist Association in Connecticut on January 1, 1802, in a letter to which he had given a great deal of thought and which he cleared through his attorney general, stated, "I contemplate with sovereign reverence that act of the whole American people which declared that their legislature should make no law respecting establishment of religion or prohibiting the free exercise thereof, thus building a wall of separation between church and state."

From that day until this most Americans and their courts of law have agreed with Jefferson's view, and the separation principle has enabled this country to achieve the world's highest levels of individual religious freedom, religious pluralism, and interfaith peace and harmony. The history of our country and of the world has amply documented the inestimable value of this principle and the genius of those who developed it.

Perhaps the most forceful explication of the First Amendment is to be found in a famous paragraph in the majority opinion in *Everson* v. *Board of Education* in 1947 (330 U.S. 15, 16), written by Justice Hugo L. Black, a statement concurred in by all of the justices: "The 'establishment of religion' clause of the First Amendment means at least this: Neither a state nor the Federal Government can set up a church. Neither can pass laws which aid one religion, aid all religions, or prefer one religion over another. Neither can force nor influence a person to go to or remain away from church against his will or force him to profess a belief or disbelief in any religion. No person can be punished for entertaining or professing religious beliefs or disbeliefs, for church attendance or non-attendance. No tax in any amount, large or small, can be levied to support any religious activities or institutions, whatever they may be called, or whatever form they may adopt to teach or practice religion. Neither a state nor the Federal Government can, openly or secretly, participate in the affairs of any religious organizations or groups and vice versa. In the words of Jefferson the clause against establishment of religion by law was intended to erect 'a wall of separation between church and state'."

Following the Civil War, Congress, recognizing that state governments had not adequately protected individual liberties, proposed the Fourteenth Amendment to the Constitution, quickly ratified by the states, which was intended to apply the Bill of Rights to state and local government. Unfortunately, the Supreme Court in the 1870s declined to accept the obvious meaning and intent of the Fourteenth Amendment, and it was not until after World War I that the Supreme Court began the piecemeal incorporation of the Bill of Rights into the Fourteenth Amendment. But that is a story beyond the purview of this book.

Attention has tended to be focussed on the national Constitution, so it is often overlooked that the state constitutions, some of which were written before the United States Constitution, include explicit protections of religious liberty and church-state separation, some even more comprehensive and specific in their guarantees and prohibitions than the federal Constitution.

State constitutions may well play an increasingly important role in defending individual freedoms and the separation principle, as a result of appointments to the U.S. Supreme Court and lower federal courts by Presidents Reagan and Bush.

This little volume brings together all of the religious liberty and church-state provisions of the fifty state constitutions. We hope it will be a useful reference work for people in the fields of education, law, and religion. We know of no comparable compilation.

We have not presented the history of the development of these constitutional provisions, nor have we presented material on the state courts' interpretations and applications of these provisions. Each of those tasks would require a hefty volume.

The reader will note that all of the state constitutions deal with religious freedom and all support the church-state separation principle. Among the interesting features of state constitutional provisions are the following:

Residents of Arkansas, Nebraska, Ohio, and Wisconsin are fortunate to live in states which have the most explicit guarantees of religious liberty. North Carolina has the fewest. Forty-six states explicitly protect freedom of worship or conscience, while thirty-five states prohibit establishment of any state religion. Twenty-nine states ban required church attendance. Thirty-one states have their own bans on religious tests for public office, while eighteen prohibit religious tests for witnesses and jurors. Forty-two states have constitutional prohibitions against appropriation of public money for religious institutions. Twenty-five states explicitly prohibit public aid for sectarian educational institutions, while the rest do so implicitly.

Sixteen states, all in the West, maintain explicit constitutional prohibitions on sectarian instruction in or sectarian control of public schools. All but three of these states entered the Union after the Civil War, and collectively they were admitted an average of 105.6 years after the federal Constitution was ratified in 1788. This shows that many states were responsive to new developments and challenges regarding the protection of individual religious liberty. These states are: Alaska, Arizona, California, Colorado, Hawaii, Idaho, Montana, Nebraska, Nevada, New Mexico, Oklahoma, South Dakota, Utah, Washington, Wisconsin, and Wyoming.

Five states (Maryland, Pennsylvania, South Carolina, Tennessee, Texas) have provisions requiring that office holders believe in a Supreme Being, but these clearly violate the U.S. Constitution, as the Supreme Court held in 1961 in *Torcaso* v. *Watkins.*

A chart providing a useful summary of state constitutional provisions on religious liberty and church-state issues may be found in Appendix I.

It is important to note, we think, that support for the church-state separation principle is not confined to any one period of our nation's history. When Congress in 1952 considered and approved the constitution of the Commonwealth of Puerto Rico, that charter not only reiterated the "no establishment" and "free exercise" clauses found in the First Amendment, but it also included the stipulation that "There shall be complete separation of church and state." And this occurred during a period in which Congress added to the existing national motto, *"E pluribus unum"* ("One from many") a new religious motto, "In God We Trust," added the phrase "under God" to the Pledge of Allegiance, and ordered the motto "In God We Trust" printed on the currency.

When Congress in 1959 approved the admission of the states of Alaska and Hawaii to the Union, it approved their constitutions, both of which include the separation principle and specifically bar the use of tax funds to aid denominational schools.

Several attempts have been made in recent years to amend state constitutions to weaken the church-state separation provisions in order to permit tax aid to or support of religious private schools. These efforts failed in Nebraska in 1966 and 1970, in New York State in 1967, in Oregon and Idaho in 1972, in Washington State in 1975, and Alaska and Missouri in 1976, in Michigan in 1978, in California in 1982, in Massachusetts in 1982 and 1986, in Oregon in 1990, and in Colorado in 1992. In 1970 supporters of church-state separation in Michigan initiated an amendment to the state constitution to strengthen the prohibition against tax aid for nonpublic education; the proposed amendment was approved 57 percent to 43 percent. In 1986 South Dakota voters approved an amendment to allow the state to provide textbooks to denominational and other nonpublic schools.

Three other significant referenda took place on the question of tax aid to church schools, in Maryland in 1972 and 1974 and in the District of Columbia in 1981. In all three cases church-state separation won. However, the referenda were on legislation, not on constitutional changes.

Edd Doerr
Albert J. Menendez
July 4, 1993

Alabama

Article I

DECLARATION OF RIGHTS

3. That no religion shall be established by law; that no preference shall be given by law to any religious sect, society, denomination or mode of worship; that no one shall be compelled by law to attend any place of worship; nor to pay tithes, taxes or other rates for building or repairing any place of worship, or for maintaining any minister or ministry; that no religious test shall be required as a qualification to any office of public trust under this State; and that the civil rights, privileges and capacities of any citizen shall not be in any manner affected by his religious principles.

Article XIV

EDUCATION

263. No money raised for the support of the public schools shall be appropriated to or used for the support of any sectarian or denominational school.

Alaska

PUBLIC DEBT, REVENUE, AND TAXATION

Section 10. No tax shall be laid or appropriation of public money made in aid of any church, or sectarian school, or any public service corporation.

Article XI

EDUCATION

Section 7. No sectarian instruction shall be imparted in any school or State educational institution that may be established under this Constitution, and no religious or political test or qualification shall ever be required as a condition of admission into any public educational institution of the State, as teacher, student, or pupil; but the liberty of conscience hereby secured shall not be so construed as to justify practices or conduct inconsistent with the good order, peace, morality, or safety of the State, or with the rights of others.

Article XX

First. Perfect toleration of religious sentiment shall be secured to every inhabitant of this State, and no inhabitant of this State shall ever be molested in person or property on account of his or her mode of religious worship, or lack of the same.

Seventh. Provisions shall be made by law for the establishment and maintenance of a system of public schools which shall be open to all the children of the State and be free from sectarian control, . . .

Arizona

Article 2

DECLARATION OF RIGHTS

Section 12. Liberty of conscience; appropriations for religious purposes prohibited; religious freedom

Section 12. The liberty of conscience secured by the provisions of this Constitution shall not be so construed as to excuse acts of licentiousness, or justify practices inconsistent with the peace and safety of the State. No public money or property shall be appropriated for or applied to any religious worship, exercise, or instruction, or to the support of any religious establishment. No religious qualification shall be required for any public office or employment, nor shall any person be incompetent as a witness or juror in consequence of his opinion on matters of religion, nor be questioned touching his religious belief in any court of justice to affect the weight of his testimony.

Article 11

Section 7. Sectarian instruction; religious or political test or qualification

Section 7. No sectarian instruction shall be imparted in any school or state educational institution that may be established under this Constitution, and no religious or political test or qualification shall ever be required as a condition of admission into any public educational institution of the State, as teacher, student, or pupil; but the liberty of conscience hereby secured shall not be so construed as to justify practices or conduct inconsistent with the good order, peace, morality, or safety of the State, or with the rights of others.

Arkansas

DECLARATION OF RIGHTS

Section 24. All men have a natural and indefeasible right to worship Almighty God according to the dictates of their own consciences; no man can, of right, be compelled to attend, erect or support any place of worship; or to maintain any ministry against his consent. No human authority can, in any case or manner whatsoever, control or interfere with the right of conscience; and no preference shall ever be given, by law, to any religious establishment, denomination or mode of worship above any other.

Section 25. Religion, morality and knowledge being essential to good government, the General Assembly shall enact suitable laws to protect every religious denomination in the peaceable enjoyment of its own mode of public worship.

Section 26. No religious test shall ever be required of any person as a qualification to vote or hold office, nor shall any person be rendered incompetent to be a witness on account of his religious belief; but nothing herein shall be construed to dispense with oaths or affirmations.

Article XIV

EDUCATION

Section 2. No money or property belonging to public school fund, or to this State for the benefit of schools or universities, shall ever be used for any other than the respective purposes to which it belongs.

California

DECLARATION OF RIGHTS

Freedom of Religion

Section 4. Free exercise and enjoyment of religion without discrimination or preference are guaranteed. This liberty of conscience does not excuse acts that are licentious or inconsistent with the peace or safety of the State. The Legislature shall make no law respecting an establishment of religion.

Article XIII

LEGISLATIVE DEPARTMENT

Public Aid for Sectarian Purposes Prohibited

Section 24. Neither the Legislature, nor any county, city and county, township, school district or other municipal corporation, shall ever make an appropriation, or pay from any public fund whatever, or grant anything to or in aid of any religious sect, church, creed, or sectarian purpose or help to support or sustain any school, college, university, hospital, or other institution controlled by any religious creed, church, or sectarian denomination whatever; nor shall any grant or donation of personal property or real estate ever be made by the State, or any city, city and county, town or other municipal corporation for any religious creed, church, or sectarian purpose whatever. . . .

Article IX

EDUCATION

No Public Money for Sectarian Schools

Section 8. No public money shall ever be appropriated for the support of any sectarian or denominational school, or any school not under the exclusive control of the officers of the public schools; nor shall any sectarian or denominational doctrine be taught, or instruction thereon be permitted, directly or indirectly, in any of the common schools of this State.

Colorado

Article II

BILL OF RIGHTS

Section 4. Religious freedom.—That the free exercise and enjoyment of religious profession and worship, without discrimination, shall forever hereafter be guaranteed; and no person shall be denied any civil or political right, privilege or capacity, on account of his opinions concerning religion; but the liberty of conscience hereby secured shall not be construed to dispense with oaths or affirmations, excuse acts of licentiousness or justify practices inconsistent with the good order, peace or safety of the state. No person shall be required to attend or support any ministry or place of worship, religious sect or denomination against his consent. Nor shall any preference be given by law to any religious denomination or mode of worship.

Article V

LEGISLATIVE DEPARTMENT

Section 34. Appropriations to private institutions forbidden. —No appropriation shall be made for charitable, industrial, educational or benevolent purposes to any person, corporation or community not under the absolute control of the state, nor to any denominational or sectarian institution or association.

Article IX

EDUCATION

Section 7. Aid to private schools, churches, etc., forbidden.— Neither the general assembly, nor any county, city, town, township, school district or other public corporation, shall ever make any appropriation, or pay from any public fund or monies whatever, anything in aid of any church or sectarian society, or for any sectarian purpose, or to help support or sustain any school, academy, seminary, college, university or other literary or scientific institution, controlled by any church or sectarian denomination whatsoever; nor shall any grant or donation of land, money or other personal property, ever be made by the state, or any such public corporation, to any church, or for any sectarian purpose.

Section 8. Religious test and race discrimination forbidden.— Sectarian tenets.—No religious test or qualification shall ever be required of any person as a condition of admission into any public educational institution of the state, either as a teacher or student; and no teacher or student of any such institution shall ever be required to attend or participate in any religious service whatever. No sectarian tenets or doctrines shall ever be taught in the public schools, . . .

Connecticut

Article First

DECLARATION OF RIGHTS

Section 3. The exercise and enjoyment of religious profession and worship, without discrimination, shall forever be free to all persons in the state; provided, that the right hereby declared and established, shall not be so construed as to excuse acts of licentiousness, or to justify practices inconsistent with the peace and safety of the state.

Article Seventh

OF RELIGION

. . . no person shall by law be compelled to join or support, nor be classed or associated with, any congregation, church or religious association. No preference shall be given by law to any religious society or denomination in the state. Each shall have and enjoy the same and equal powers, rights and privileges, and may support and maintain the ministers and teachers of its society or denomination, and may build and repair houses for public worship.

Delaware

Article I

BILL OF RIGHTS

1. *Freedom of Religion*

Section I. Although it is the duty of all men frequently to assemble together for the public worship of Almighty God; and piety and morality, on which the prosperity of communities depends are hereby promoted; yet no man shall or ought to be compelled to attend any religious worship, to contribute to the erection or support of any place of worship, or to the maintenance of any ministry, against his own free will and consent; and no power shall or ought to be vested in or assumed by any magistrate that shall in any case interfere with, or in any manner control the rights of conscience, in the free exercise of religious worship, nor a preference given by law to any religious societies, denominations, or modes of worship.

Article X

EDUCATION

Section 3. No portion of any fund now existing or which may hereafter be appropriated, or raised by tax, for educational purposes, shall be appropriated to, or used by, or in aid of any sectarian, church or denominational school; . . .

4. *Use of Public School Fund*

Section 4. No part of the principal or income of the Public School Fund, now or hereafter existing, shall be used for any other purpose than the support of free public schools.

Florida

Article I

Section 3. There shall be no law respecting the establishment of religion or prohibiting or penalizing the free exercise thereof. Religious freedom shall not justify practices inconsistent with public morals, peace or safety. No revenue of the state or any political subdivision or agency thereof shall ever be taken from the public treasury or indirectly in aid of any church, sect, or religious denomination or in aid of any sectarian institution.

Georgia

Article I

BILL OF RIGHTS

Section I

Section 2-102, Paragraph XII. Freedom of conscience. All men have the natural and inalienable right to worship God, each according to the dictates of his own conscience, and no human authority should, in any case, control or interfere with such right of conscience.

Section 2-103, Paragraph XIII. Religious opinions; liberty of conscience. No inhabitant of this State shall be molested in person or property, or prohibited from holding any public office, or trust, on account of his religious opinions; but the right of liberty of conscience shall not be so construed as to excuse acts of licentiousness, or justify practices inconsistent with the peace and safety of the State.

Hawaii

Article I

BILL OF RIGHTS

Freedom of Religion, Speech, Press, Assembly and Petition

Section 3. No law shall be enacted respecting an establishment of religion or prohibiting the free exercise thereof, . . .

Article IX

EDUCATION

Public Education

Section 1. The State shall provide for the establishment, support and control of a statewide system of public schools free from sectarian control, a state university, public libraries and such other educational institutions as may be deemed desirable, including physical facilities therefor. There shall be no segregation in public educational institutions because of race, religion or ancestry; nor shall public funds be appropriated for the support or benefit of any sectarian or private educational institution.

Idaho

Article IX

EDUCATION AND SCHOOL LANDS

5. Sectarian appropriations prohibited.—Neither the legislature nor any county, city, town, township, school district, or other public corporation, shall ever make any appropriation, or pay from any public fund or monies whatever, anything in aid of any church or sectarian or religious society, or for any sectarian or religious purpose, or to help support or sustain any school, academy, seminary, college, university, or other literary or scientific institution, controlled by any church, sectarian or religious denomination whatsoever; nor shall any grant or donation of land, money or other personal property ever be made by the state, or any such public corporation, to any church or for any sectarian or religious purpose.

6. Religious test and teaching school prohibited.—No religious test or qualification shall ever be required of any person as a condition of admission into any public educational institution of the state, either as teacher or student; and no teacher or student of any such institution shall ever be required to attend or participate in any religious service whatever. No sectarian or religious tenets or doctrines shall ever be taught in the public schools, nor shall

any distinction or classification of pupils be made on account of race or color. No books, papers, tracts or documents of a political, sectarian or denominational character shall be used or introduced in any schools established under the provisions of this article, nor shall any teacher or any district receive any of the public school monies in which the schools have not been taught in accordance with the provisions of this article.

Illinois

Article I

BILL OF RIGHTS

Inherent and Inalienable Rights.

Religious Freedom.

Section 3. The free exercise and enjoyment of religious profession and worship, without discrimination, shall forever be guaranteed; and no person shall be denied any civil or political right, privilege or capacity, on account of his religious opinions; but the liberty of the conscience hereby secured shall not be construed to dispense with oaths or affirmations, excuse acts of licentiousness, or justify practices inconsistent with the peace or safety of the State. No person shall be required to attend or support any ministry or place of worship against his consent, nor shall any preference be given by law to any religious denomination or mode of worship.

Public Funds for Sectarian Purposes Forbidden.

Section 3. Neither the General Assembly nor any county, city, town, township, school district, or other public corporation, shall ever make any appropriation or pay from any public fund whatever, anything in aid of any church or sectarian purpose, or to help support or sustain any school, academy, seminary, college, university, or other literary or scientific institution, controlled by any church or sectarian denomination whatever; nor shall any grant or donation of land, money, or other personal property ever be made by the State, or any such public corporation, to any church or for any sectarian purpose.

Indiana

Article I

BILL OF RIGHTS

Section 2. All men shall be secured in the natural right to worship Almighty God, according to the dictates of their own consciences.

Section 3. No law shall, in any case whatever, control the free exercise and enjoyment of religious opinions, or interfere with the rights of conscience.

Section 4. No preference shall be given, by law, to any creed, religious society, or mode of worship; and no man shall be compelled to attend, erect, or support, any place of worship, or to maintain any ministry, against his consent.

Section 5. No religious test shall be required, as a qualification for any office of trust or profit.

Section 6. No money shall be drawn from the treasury, for the benefit of any religious or theological institution.

Section 7. No person shall be rendered incompetent as a witness, in consequence of his opinions on matters of religion.

Iowa

Article I

BILL OF RIGHTS

Section 3. The General Assembly shall make no law respecting an establishment of religion, or prohibiting the free exercise thereof; nor shall any person be compelled to attend any place of worship, pay tithes, taxes or other rates for building or repairing places of worship, or the maintenance of any minister, or ministry.

Section 4. No religious test shall be required as a qualification for any office or public trust, and no person shall be deprived of any of his rights, privileges, or capacities, or disqualified from the performance of any of his public or private duties, or rendered incompetent to give evidence in any court of law or equity, in consequence of his opinions on the subject of religion; . . .

Kansas

BILL OF RIGHTS

7. Religious liberty. The right to worship God according to the dictates of conscience shall never be infringed; nor shall any control of or interference with the rights of conscience be permitted, nor any preference be given by law to any religious establishment or mode of worship. No religious test or property qualification shall be required for any office of public trust, nor for any vote at any election, nor shall any person be incompetent to testify on account of religious belief.

Article VI

EDUCATION

6.(c). No religious sect or sects shall control any part of the public educational funds.

Kentucky

BILL OF RIGHTS

Second: The right of worshiping Almighty God according to the dictates of their consciences.

Section 5. Right of religious freedom. No preference shall ever be given by law to any religious sect, society or denomination; nor to any particular creed, mode of worship or system of ecclesiastical polity; nor shall any person be compelled to attend any place of worship, to contribute to the erection or maintenance of any such place, or to the salary or support of any minister of religion; nor shall any man be compelled to send his child to any school to which he may be conscientiously opposed; and the civil rights, privileges or capacities of no person shall be taken away, or in anywise diminished or enlarged, on account of his belief or disbelief of any religious tenet, dogma or teaching. No human authority shall in any case whatever, control or interfere with the rights of conscience.

Louisiana

BILL OF RIGHTS

4. Freedom of Religion

Section 4. Every person has the natural right to worship God according to the dictates of his own conscience. No law shall be passed respecting an establishment of religion, nor prohibiting the free exercise thereof; nor shall any preference ever be given to, nor any discrimination be made against, any church, sect, or creed of religion, or any form of religious faith or worship.

Article IV

Section 8. No money shall ever be taken from the public treasury, directly or indirectly, in aid of any church, sect or denomination of religion, or in aid of any priest, preacher, minister or teacher thereof, as such, and no preference shall ever be given to, nor any discrimination made against, any church, sect or creed of religion, or any form of religious faith or worship.

Article XII

Section 13. No appropriation of public funds shall be made to any private or sectarian school.

Article XIV

Section 15(A)(1). . . . no person in the State or City Classified Service shall be discriminated against or subjected to any disciplinary action for political or religious reasons, and all such persons shall have the right of appeal from such action.

Maine

DECLARATION OF RIGHTS

Religious freedom.

Section 3. All men have a natural and unalienable right to worship Almighty God according to the dictates of their own consciences, and no one shall be hurt, molested or restrained in his person, liberty or estate for worshiping God in the manner and season most agreeable to the dictates of his own conscience, nor for his religious professions or sentiments, provided he does not disturb the public peace, nor obstruct others in their religious worship;—and all persons demeaning themselves peaceably, as good members of the state, shall be equally under the protection of the laws, and no subordination nor preference of any one sect or denomination to another shall ever be established by law, "nor shall any religious test be required as a qualification for any office or trust," under this State; . . .

Maryland

DECLARATION OF RIGHTS

Article 36. That as it is the duty of every man to worship God in such a manner as he thinks most acceptable to Him, all persons are equally entitled to protection in their religious liberty; wherefore, no person ought by any law to be molested in his person or estate, on account of his religious persuasion, or profession, or for his religious practice, unless, under the color of religion, he shall disturb the good order, peace or safety of the State, or shall infringe the laws of morality, or injure others in their natural, civil or religious rights; nor ought any person to be compelled to frequent, or maintain, or contribute, unless on contract, to maintain any place of worship, or any ministry; nor shall any person, otherwise competent, be deemed incompetent as a witness, or juror, on account of his religious belief; provided, he believes in the existence of God, and that under His dispensation such person will be held morally accountable for his acts, and be rewarded or punished therefor either in this world or in the world to come.

Nothing shall prohibit or require the making reference to belief in, reliance upon, or invoking the aid of God or a Supreme Being in any governmental or public document, proceeding, activity, ceremony, school institution, or place.

Nothing in this article shall constitute an establishment of religion.

Article 37. That religious test ought never to be required as a qualification for any office of profit or trust in this State, other than a declaration of belief in the existence of God, . . .[1]

---

1. Invalidated by the U.S. Supreme Court in *Torcaso* v. *Watkins* 367 US 495 (1961).

Massachusetts

A DECLARATION OF THE RIGHTS OF THE INHABITANTS OF THE COMMONWEALTH OF MASSACHUSETTS

II. . . . no Subject shall be hurt, molested, or restrained, in his person, Liberty, or Estate, for worshipping God in the manner and season most agreeable to the Dictates of his own conscience, or for his religious beliefs.

Religious Societies.

Article III. . . . the several religious societies of this Commonwealth, whether corporate or unincorporate, at any meeting legally warned and holden for that purpose, shall ever have the right to elect their pastors or religious teachers, to contract with them for their support to raise money for erecting and repairing houses for public worship, for the maintenance of religious instruction and for the payment of necessary expenses; . . . all religious sects and denominations demeaning themselves peaceably and as good citizens of the Commonwealth, shall be equally under the protection of the law; and no subordination of any one sect or denomination to another shall ever be established by law.

Article XVIII

Section 1. No law shall be passed prohibiting the free exercise of religion.

Section 2. No grant, appropriation of the use of public money or property or loan of credit shall be made or authorized by the Commonwealth or any political subdivision thereof for the purpose of founding, maintaining or aiding any infirmary, hospital, institution, primary or secondary school, or charitable or religious undertaking which is not publicly owned and under the exclusive control, order and supervision of public officers or public agents authorized by the Commonwealth . . . no such grant, appropriation or use of public money or property or loan of public credit shall be made or authorized for the purpose of founding, maintaining or aiding any church, religious denomination or society.

Section 4. Nothing herein contained shall be construed to deprive any inmate of a publicly controlled reformatory, penal or charitable institution of the opportunity of religious exercises therein of his own faith; but no inmate of such institution shall be compelled to attend religious services or receive religious instruction against his will, or, if a minor, without the consent of his parent or guardian.

Michigan

DECLARATION OF RIGHTS

Section 4. Every person shall be at liberty to worship God according to the dictates of his own conscience. No person shall be compelled to attend, or against his consent, to contribute to the erection or support of any place of religious worship, or to pay tithes, taxes or other rates for the support of any minister of the gospel or teacher of religion. No money shall be appropriated or drawn from the treasury for the benefit of any religious sect or society, theological or religious seminary; nor shall property belonging to the state be appropriated for any such purpose. The civil and political rights, privileges and capacities of no person shall be diminished or enlarged on account of his religious belief.

Article VIII

EDUCATION

Section 2. . . . Every school district shall provide for the education of its pupils without discrimination as to religion, creed, race, color or national origin.

No public monies or property shall be appropriated or paid or any public credit utilized, by the legislature or any other political subdivision or agency of the state directly or indirectly to aid or maintain any private, denominational or other nonpublic preelementary, elementary, or secondary school. No payment, credit, tax benefit, exemption of deductions, tuition voucher, subsidy, grant or loan of public monies or property shall be provided, directly or indirectly, to support the attendance of any student or the employment of any person at any such nonpublic school or at any location or institution where instruction is offered in whole or in part to such nonpublic school students. . . .

Minnesota

Article I

BILL OF RIGHTS

Section 16. The enumeration of rights in this constitution shall not be construed to deny or impair others retained by and inherent in the people. The right of every man to worship God according to the dictates of his own conscience shall never be infringed, nor shall any man be compelled to attend, erect or support any place of worship, or to maintain any religious or ecclesiastical ministry, against his consent; nor shall any control of or interference with the rights of conscience be permitted or any preference be given by law to any religious establishment or mode of worship; but the liberty of conscience hereby secured shall not be so construed as to excuse acts of licentiousness, or justify practices inconsistent with the peace or safety of the State, nor shall any money be drawn from the treasury for the benefit of any religious societies or religious or theological seminaries.

Section 17. No religious test or amount of property shall ever be required as a qualification for any office of public trust under the State. No religious test or amount of property shall ever be required as a qualification of any voter at any election in this State; nor shall any person be rendered incompetent to give evidence in any court of law or equity in consequence of his opinion upon the subject of religion.

Article XIII

Section 2. In no case shall any public money or property be appropriated or used for the support of schools wherein the distinctive doctrines, creeds or tenets of any particular Christian or other religious sect are promulgated or taught.

Mississippi

Article III

Section 18. No religious test as a qualification for office shall be required; and no preference shall be given by law to any religious sect or mode of worship; but the free enjoyment of all religious sentiments and the different modes of worship shall be held sacred. The rights hereby secured shall not be construed to justify acts of licentiousness injurious to morals or dangerous to the peace and safety of the state, or to exclude the Holy Bible from use in any public school of this state.

Article VIII

Section 208. No religious or other sect or sects shall ever control any part of the school or other educational funds of this state; nor shall any funds be appropriated toward the support of any sectarian school, or to any school that at the time of receiving such appropriation is not conducted as a free school.

Missouri

Article I

BILL OF RIGHTS

Section 5. Religious freedom—liberty of conscience and belief—limitations.—That all men have a natural and indefeasible right to worship Almighty God according to the dictates of their own consciences; that no human authority can control or interfere with the rights of conscience; that no person shall, on account of his religious persuasion or belief, be rendered ineligible to any public office or trust or profit in this state, be disqualified from testifying or serving as a juror, or be molested in his person or estate; . . .

Section 6. That no person can be compelled to erect, support or attend any place or system of worship, or to maintain or support any priest, minister, preacher or teacher of any sect, church, creed or denomination of religion; . . .

Section 7. That no money shall ever be taken from the public treasury, directly or indirectly, in aid of any church, sect or denomination of religion, or in aid of any priest, preacher, minister or teacher thereof, as such; and that no preference shall be given to nor any discrimination made against any church, sect or creed of religion, or any form of religious faith or worship.

Article IX

EDUCATION

Section 8. Neither the general assembly, nor any county, city, town, township, school district or other municipal corporation, shall ever make an appropriation or pay from any public fund whatever, anything in aid of any religious creed, church or sectarian purpose or to help to support or sustain any private or public school, academy, seminary, college, university, or other institution of learning controlled by any religious creed, church or sectarian denomination whatever; nor shall any grant of donation, personal property or real estate ever be made by the state, or any county, city, town, or other municipal corporation, for any religious creed, church, or sectarian purpose whatever.

Montana

DECLARATION OF RIGHTS

Section 5. Freedom of religion.—The state shall make no law respecting an establishment of religion or prohibiting the free exercise thereof.

Article X

EDUCATION AND PUBLIC LANDS

Section 6. Aid prohibited to sectarian schools.
(1) The legislature, counties, cities, towns, school districts, and public corporations shall not make any direct or indirect appropriation or payment from any public fund or monies, or any grant of lands or other property for any sectarian purpose or to aid any church, school, academy, seminary, college, university, or other literary or scientific institution, controlled in whole or in part by any church, sect, or denomination.
(2) This section shall not apply to funds from federal sources

provided to the state for the express purpose of distribution to non-public education.

Section 7. Non-discrimination in education. No religious or partisan test or qualification shall be required of any teacher or student as a condition of admission into any public educational institution. Attendance shall not be required at any religious service. No sectarian tenets shall be advocated in any public educational institution of the state. No person shall be refused admission to any public educational institution on account of sex, race, creed, religion, political beliefs, or national origin.

Nebraska

BILL OF RIGHTS

Section 4. All persons have a natural and indefeasible right to worship Almighty God according to the dictates of their own consciences. No person shall be compelled to attend, erect or support any place of worship against his consent, and no preference shall be given by law to any religious society, nor shall any interference with the rights of conscience be permitted. No religious test shall be required as a qualification for office, nor shall any person be incompetent to be a witness on account of his religious beliefs; but nothing herein shall be construed to dispense with oaths and affirmations. Religion, morality, and knowledge, however, being essential to good government, it shall be the duty of the Legislature to pass suitable laws to protect every religious denomination in the peaceable enjoyment of its own mode of public worship, and to encourage schools and the means of instruction.

Article VII

EDUCATION

Section 11. All public schools shall be free of sectarian instruction. A religious test or qualification shall not be required of any teacher or student for admission or continuance in any school or institution supported in whole or in part by public funds or taxation.

Nevada

Article I

DECLARATION OF RIGHTS

Section 4. The free exercise and enjoyment of religious profession and worship, without discrimination or preference, shall forever be allowed [in] this state; and no person shall be rendered incompetent to be a witness on account of his opinions on matters of his religious belief; but the liberty of conscience hereby secured shall not be so construed as to excuse acts of licentiousness, or justify practices inconsistent with the peace, or safety of this state.

Article XI

EDUCATION

Section 2. . . . any school district which shall allow instruction of a sectarian character therein may be deprived of its proportion of the interest of the public school fund during such neglect or infraction . . .

Section 9. No sectarian instruction shall be imparted or tolerated in any school or university that may be established under this constitution.

Section 10. No public funds of any kind or character whatever, state, county, or municipal, shall be used for sectarian purposes.

New Hampshire

BILL OF RIGHTS

5th. Every individual has a natural and unalienable right to worship God according to the dictates of his own conscience, and reason; and no subject shall be hurt, molested or restrained, in his person, liberty, or estate, for worshipping God in the manner and season most agreeable to the dictates of his own conscience, or for his religious profession, sentiments, or persuasion; provided he doth not disturb the public peace or disturb others in their religious worship.

6th. . . . the several parishes, bodies corporate, or religious societies shall at all times have the right of electing their own teachers, and of contracting with them for their support or maintenance, or both. But no person shall ever be compelled to pay towards the support of the schools of any sect or denomination. And every person, denomination or sect shall be equally under the protection of the law and no subordination of any one sect, denomination or persuasion to another shall ever be established.

Article 83

. . . no money raised by taxation shall ever be granted or applied for the use of the schools or institutions of any religious sect or denomination.

New Jersey

Article I

RIGHTS AND PRIVILEGES

3. No person shall be deprived of the inestimable privilege of worshipping Almighty God in a manner agreeable to the dictates of his own conscience; nor under any pretense whatever be compelled to attend any place of worship contrary to his faith and judgment; nor shall any person be obliged to pay tithes, taxes, or other rates for building or repairing any church or churches, place or places of worship, or for the maintenance of any minister or ministry, contrary to what he believes to be right or has deliberately and voluntarily engaged to perform.

4. There shall be no establishment of one religious sect in preference to another; no religious or racial test shall be required as a qualification for any office or public trust.

5. No person shall be denied the enjoyment of any civil or military right, nor be discriminated against in the exercise of any civil or military right, nor be segregated in the militia or in the public schools, because of religious principles, race, color, ancestry or national origin.

New Mexico

Article II

BILL OF RIGHTS

Section 11. Every man shall be free to worship God to the dictates of his own conscience, and no person shall ever be molested or denied any civil or political right or privilege on account of his religious opinion or mode of religious worship. No person shall be required to attend any place of worship or support any religious sect or denomination; nor shall any preference be given by law to any religious denomination or mode of worship.

Article IV

Section 31. No appropriation shall be made for charitable, educational or other benevolent purposes to any person, corporation, association, institution or community, not under the absolute control of the state. . . .

Article XII

EDUCATION

Section 3. . . . no part of the proceeds arising from the sale or disposal of any lands granted to the State by Congress, or any other funds appropriated, levied or collected for educational purposes, shall be used for the support of any sectarian, denominational or private school, college or university.

Section 9. No religious test shall ever be required as a condition of admission into the public schools or any educational institution of this State, either as a teacher or student and no teacher or students of such school or institution shall ever be required to attend or participate in any religious service whatsoever.

Article XXI

COMPACT WITH THE UNITED STATES

Section 1. Religious toleration—Polygamy.—Perfect toleration of religious sentiment shall be secured, and no inhabitant of this state shall ever be molested in person or property on account of his or her mode of religious worship. Polygamous or plural marriages and polygamous cohabitation are forever prohibited.

New York

Article I

BILL OF RIGHTS

Section 3. The free exercise and enjoyment of religious professions and worship, without discrimination or preference, shall forever be allowed in this state to all mankind; and no person shall be rendered incompetent to be a witness on account of his opinions on matters of religious belief; but the liberty of conscience hereby secured shall not be so construed as to excuse acts of licentiousness, or justify practices inconsistent with the peace or safety of this state.

Article XI

EDUCATION

Section 3. Neither the state nor any subdivision thereof shall use its property or credit or any public money, or authorize or permit either to be used, directly or indirectly, in aid or maintenance, other than for examination or inspection, of any school or institution of learning wholly or in part under the control or direction of any religious denomination, or in which any denominational tenet or doctrine is taught, but the legislature may provide for the transportation of children to and from any school or institution of learning.

North Carolina

Article I

DECLARATION OF RIGHTS

Section 13. Religious liberty. All persons have a natural and inalienable right to worship Almighty God according to the dictates of their own consciences, and no human authority should, in any case whatever, control or interfere with the rights of conscience.

North Dakota

Article I

DECLARATION OF RIGHTS

Section 4. The free exercise and enjoyment of religious profession and worship, without discrimination or preference, shall be forever guaranteed in this state, and no person shall be rendered incompetent to be a witness or juror on account of his opinion on matters of religious belief; but the liberty of conscience hereby secured shall not be so construed as to excuse acts of licentiousness, or justify practices inconsistent with the peace or safety of this state.

Article VIII

EDUCATION

Section 147. . . . the legislative assembly shall make provision for the establishment and maintenance of a system of public schools which shall be open to all children of the state of North Dakota and free from sectarian control.

Section 152. . . . No money raised for the support of the public schools of the state shall be appropriated to or used for support of any sectarian school.

Article XVI

COMPACT WITH THE UNITED STATES

Section 203. Perfect toleration of religious sentiment shall be secured, no inhabitant of this state shall ever be molested in person or property on account of his or her mode of religious worship.

Ohio

BILL OF RIGHTS

7. *Rights of conscience* . . .

All men have a natural and indefeasible right to worship Almighty God according to the dictates of their own conscience. No person shall be compelled to attend, erect, or support any place of worship, or maintain any form of worship, against his consent; and no preference shall be given, by law, to any religious society; nor shall any interference with the rights of conscience be permitted. No religious test shall be required, as a qualification for office, nor shall any person be incompetent to be a witness on account of his religious belief; but nothing herein shall be construed to dispense with oaths and affirmations. Religion, morality, and knowledge, however, being essential to good government, it shall be the duty of the General Assembly to pass suitable laws, to protect every religious denomination in the peaceable enjoyment of its own mode of public worship, and to encourage schools and the means of instruction.

Article VI

EDUCATION

2.

. . . no religious or other sect, or sects, shall ever have any exclusive right to, or control of, any part of the school funds of this State.

Oklahoma

Article I

FEDERAL RELATIONS

2.

Perfect toleration of religious sentiment shall be secured, and no inhabitant of the State shall ever be molested in person or property on account of his or her mode of religious worship, and no religious test shall be required for the exercise of civil or political rights, polygamous or plural marriages are forever prohibited.

5. *Public schools* . . .

Provisions shall be made for the establishment and maintenance of a system of public schools, which shall be open to all the children of the State and free from sectarian control . . .

Article II

BILL OF RIGHTS

5.

No public money or property shall ever be appropriated, applied, donated, or used, directly or indirectly, for the use, benefit or support of any sect, church, denomination, or system of religion, or for the use, benefit or support of any priest, preacher, minister, or other religious teacher or dignitary, or sectarian institution as such.

Oregon

Article I

Section 2. Freedom of worship. All men shall be secure in the Natural right, to worship Almighty God according to the dictates of their own consciences.

Section 3. Freedom of religious opinion. No law shall in any case whatever control the free exercise, and enjoyment of religious opinions, or interfere with the rights of conscience.

Section 4. No religious qualification for office. No religious test shall be required as a qualification for any office of trust or profit.

Section 5. No money to be appropriated for religion. No money shall be drawn from the Treasury for the benefit of any religious, or theological institution, nor shall any money be appropriated for the payment of any religious services in either house of the Legislative Assembly.

Section 6. No religious test for witnesses or jurors. No person shall be rendered incompetent as a witness, or juror in consequence of his opinions on matters of religion; nor be questioned in any Court of Justice touching his religious belief to affect the weight of his testimony.

Pennsylvania

Article I

DECLARATION OF RIGHTS

Religious Freedom

Section 3. All men have a natural and indefeasible right to worship Almighty God according to the dictates of their own consciences; no man can of right be compelled to attend, erect or support any place of worship, or to maintain any ministry against his consent; no human authority can, in any case whatever, control or interfere with the rights of conscience, and no preference shall ever be given by law to any religious establishment or modes of worship.

Religion

Section 4. No person who acknowledges the being of a God and a future state of rewards and punishments shall, on account of his religious sentiments, be disqualified to hold any office or place of trust or profit under this Commonwealth.[2]

---

2. Presumably invalid under *Torcaso* v. *Watkins*.

Article III

LEGISLATION

Section 15. Public school money not available to sectarian schools.

No money raised for support of the public schools for the Commonwealth shall be appropriated to or used for the support of any sectarian school.

Section 29. No appropriation shall be made for charitable, educational and benevolent purposes to any person or community nor to any denominational and sectarian institution, corporation or association: . . . no scholarship, grants or loans for higher educational purposes shall be given to persons enrolled in a theological seminary or school of theology.

Rhode Island

Section 3. Whereas Almighty God hath created the mind free; and all attempts to influence it by temporal punishments or burdens, or by civil incapacitations, tend to beget habits of hypocrisy and meanness; and whereas a principal object of our venerable ancestors, in their migration to this country and their settlement of this state, was, as they expressed it, to hold forth a lively experiment, that a flourishing civil state may stand and be best maintained with full liberty in religious concernments: We, therefore, declare that no man shall be compelled to frequent or to support any religious worship, place, or ministry whatever, except in fulfillment of his own voluntary contract; nor enforced, restrained, molested, or burdened in his body or goods; nor disqualified from holding any office; nor otherwise suffer on account of his religious belief; and that every man shall be free to worship God according to the dictates of his own conscience, and to profess and by argument to maintain his opinion in matters of religion; and that the same shall in no wise diminish, enlarge, or affect his civil capacity.

South Carolina

Article I

DECLARATION OF RIGHTS

Section 2. . . . The General Assembly shall make no law respecting an establishment of religion or prohibiting the free exercise thereof . . .

Article XI

PUBLIC EDUCATION

Section 4. Direct aid to religious or other private educational institutions prohibited.

No money shall be paid from public funds nor shall the credit of the State or any of its political subdivisions be used for the direct benefit of any religious or other private educational institution.

Section 4. Supreme Being—No person who denies the existence of a Supreme Being shall hold any office under this Constitution.[3]

---

3. Presumably invalid under *Torcaso* v. *Watkins.*

South Dakota

Article VI

BILL OF RIGHTS

Section 3. The right to worship God according to the dictates of conscience shall never be infringed. No person shall be denied any civil or political right, privilege or position on account of his religion but the liberty of conscience hereby secured shall not be so construed as to excuse licentiousness, the invasion of the rights of others, or justify practices inconsistent with the peace or safety of the state.

No person shall be compelled to attend or support any ministry or place of worship against his consent nor shall any preference be given by law to any religious establishment or mode of worship. No money or property of the state shall be given or appropriated for the benefit of any sectarian or religious society or institution.

Article VIII

EDUCATION AND SCHOOL LANDS

Section 16. No appropriation of lands, money or other property or credits to aid any sectarian school shall ever be made by the state, or any county or municipality within the state, nor shall the state or any county or municipality within the state accept any grant, conveyance, gift, or bequest, of lands, money or other property to be used for sectarian purposes, and no sectarian instruction shall be allowed in any school or institution aided or supported by the state.

Article XXII

Fourth. That provision shall be made for the establishment and maintenance of systems of public schools, which shall be open for all the children of this state, and free from sectarian control.

Tennessee

Article I

DECLARATION OF RIGHTS

Section 3. Freedom of Worship.—That all men have a natural and indefeasible right to worship Almighty God according to the dictates of their own conscience; that no man can of right be compelled to attend, erect, or support any place of worship, or to maintain any minister against his consent; that no human authority can, in any case whatever control or interfere with the rights of conscience; and that no preference shall ever be given, by law to any religious establishment or mode of worship.

Section 4. No religious or political test.—That no political or religious test, other than an oath to support the Constitution of the United States and of this State, shall ever be required as a qualification to any office or public trust under this state.

Article IX

Section 2. . . . No person who denies the being of God, or a future state of rewards and punishments, shall hold any office in the civil department of the State.[4]

Section 15. Religious holidays.—No person shall in time of peace be required to perform any service to the public on any day set apart by his religion as a day of rest.

---

4. Presumably invalid under *Torcaso* v. *Watkins.*

Texas

Article I

BILL OF RIGHTS

Section 4. There Shall Be No Religious Test for Office.—
No religious test shall ever be required as a qualification to any
office or public trust in this State; nor shall anyone be excluded
from holding office on account of his religious sentiments, provided
he acknowledge the existence of a Supreme Being.[5]

Section 5. . . . No person shall be disqualified to give evidence
in any of the courts of this State on account of his religious opinions,
or for want of any religious belief . . . .

Section 6. Freedom in Religious Worship Guaranteed.—All
men have a natural and indefeasible right to worship Almighty
God according to the dictates of their own consciences. No man
shall be compelled to attend, erect or support any place of worship,
or to maintain any ministry against his consent. No human authority
ought, in any case whatever, to control or interfere with the rights
of conscience in matters of religion, and no preference shall ever
be given by law to any religious society or mode of worship. But

---

5. Presumably invalid under *Torcaso* v. *Watkins*.

it shall be the duty of the Legislature to pass such laws as may be necessary to protect equally every religious denomination in the peaceable enjoyment of its own mode of public worship.

Section 7. No appropriation for Sectarian Purposes. No money shall be appropriated or drawn from the Treasury for the benefit of any sect, or religious society, theological or religious seminary, nor shall property belonging to the State be appropriated for any such purposes.

Article VII

Section 5. . . . no law shall ever be enacted appropriating any part of the permanent or available school fund to any other purpose whatever; nor shall the same, or any part thereof ever be appropriated to or used for the support any sectarian school . . .

Utah

Article I

DECLARATION OF RIGHTS

Section 4. (*Religious liberty*)

The rights of conscience shall never be infringed. The State shall make no law respecting an establishment of religion or prohibiting the free exercise thereof; no religious test shall be required as a qualification for any office of public trust or for any vote at any election; nor shall any person be incompetent as a witness or juror on account of religious belief or the absence thereof. There shall be no union of Church and State, nor shall any church dominate the State or interfere with its functions. No public money or property shall be appropriated for or applied to any religious worship, exercise or instruction, or for the support of any ecclesiastical establishment. . . .

Article III

First:—Perfect toleration of religious sentiment is guaranteed. No inhabitant of this State shall ever be molested in person or property on account of his or her mode of religious worship; but polygamous or plural marriages are forever prohibited.

Fourth:—The Legislature shall make laws for the establishment and maintenance of a system of public schools, which shall be open to all the children of the State and be free from sectarian control.

Article X

EDUCATION

Section 2.

The Legislature shall provide for the establishment and maintenance of a uniform system of public schools, which shall be open to all children of the State, and be free from sectarian control.

Section 12. (*No religious or partisan tests in schools.*)

Neither religious nor partisan test or qualification shall be required of any person as a condition of admission, as teacher or student, into any public institution in the State.

Section 13. (*Public aid to church schools forbidden.*)

Neither the Legislature nor any county, city, town, school district or other public corporation, shall make any appropriation to aid in the support of any school, seminary, academy, college, university or other institution, controlled in whole, or in part, by any church sect or denomination whatever.

Vermont

Chapter I

A Declaration of the Rights of the Inhabitants of the State of Vermont

Article 3rd. That all men have a natural and unalienable right, to worship Almighty God, according to the dictates of their own consciences and understandings, as in their opinion shall be regulated by the word of God; and that no man ought to, or of right can be compelled to attend any religious worship, or erect or support any place of worship, or maintain any minister, contrary to the dictates of his conscience nor can any man be justly deprived or abridged of any civil right as a citizen, on account of his religious sentiments, or peculiar mode of religious worship; and that no authority can, or ought to be vested in, or assumed by, any power whatever, that shall in any case interfere with, or in any manner control the rights of conscience, in the free exercise of religious worship. Nevertheless, every sect or denomination of Christians ought to observe the sabbath or Lord's day, and keep up some sort of religious worship, which to them shall seem most agreeable to the revealed will of God.

Chapter II

Section 68. . . . All religious societies, or bodies of men that may be united or incorporated for the advancement of religion and learning, or for other pious and charitable purposes, shall be encouraged and protected in the enjoyment of the privileges, immunities, and estates, which they in justice ought to enjoy . . .

Virginia

BILL OF RIGHTS

Article I

Section 16. Free exercise of religion; no establishment of religion. That religion or the duty which we owe to our Creator, and the manner of discharging it, can be directed only be reason and conviction, not by force or violence; and, therefore, all men are equally entitled to the free exercise of religion, according to the dictates of conscience; and that it is the mutual duty of all to practice Christian forbearance, love, and charity towards each other. No man shall be compelled to frequent or support any religious worship, place, or ministry whatsoever, nor shall be enforced, restrained, molested, or burthened in his body or goods, nor shall otherwise suffer on account of his religious opinions or belief; but all men shall be free to profess and by argument to maintain their opinions in matters of religion, and the same shall in no wise diminish, enlarge, or affect their civil capacities. And the General Assembly shall not prescribe any religious test whatever, or confer any peculiar privileges or advantages on any sect or denomination, or pass any law requiring or authorizing any religious society, or the people of any district within the Commonwealth, to levy on themselves or others, any tax for the erection or repair of any house of public worship, or for the support of any church or ministry; but it shall be left free to every person to select his religious instructor, and to make for his support such private contract as he shall please.

Article IV

Section 16. Appropriations to religious or charitable bodies. The General Assembly shall not make any appropriation of public funds, personal property, or real estate to any church or sectarian society, or any association or institution of any kind whatever which is entirely or partly, directly or indirectly, controlled by any church or sectarian society. . . .

Washington

DECLARATION OF RIGHTS

Article I

Section 11. Religious Freedom. Absolute freedom of conscience in all matters of religious sentiment, belief and worship, shall be guaranteed to every individual, and no one shall be molested or disturbed in person or property on account of religion; but the liberty of conscience hereby secured shall not be so construed as to excuse acts of licentiousness or justify practices inconsistent with the peace and safety of the state. No public money or property shall be appropriated for or applied to any religious worship, exercise or instruction, or the support of any religious establishment: Provided, however, That this article shall not be so construed as to forbid the employment by the state of a chaplain for such of the state custodial, correctional and mental institutions as in the discretion of the legislature may seem justified. No religious qualification shall be required for any public office or employment, nor shall any person be incompetent as a witness or juror, in consequence of his opinion on matters of religion, nor be questioned in any court of justice touching his religious belief to affect the weight of his testimony.

Article IX

EDUCATION

Section 4. Sectarian Control or Influence Prohibited. All schools maintained or supported wholly or in part by the public funds shall be forever free from sectarian control or influence.

Article XXVI

First: That perfect toleration of religious sentiment shall be secured and that no inhabitant of this State shall ever be molested in person or property on account of his or her mode of religious worship.

West Virginia

Article III

BILL OF RIGHTS

Religious Freedom Guaranteed

15. No man shall be compelled to frequent or support any religious worship, place or ministry whatsoever; nor shall any man be enforced, restrained, or molested or burthened, in his body or goods, or otherwise suffer, on account of his religious opinions or beliefs, but all men shall be free to profess, and, by argument, to maintain their opinions in matters of religion; and the same shall, in no wise, affect, diminish or enlarge their civil capacities; and the Legislature shall not prescribe any religious test whatever, or confer any peculiar privileges or advantages on any sect or denomination, or pass any law requiring or authorizing any religious society, or the people of any district within this State, to levy on themselves, or others, any tax for the erection or repair of any house of public worship, or for the support of any church or ministry, but it shall be left free for every person to select his religious instructor, and to make for his support private contracts as he shall please.

Wisconsin

Article I

BILL OF RIGHTS

Section 18. The right of every man to worship Almighty God according to the dictates of his own conscience shall never be infringed; nor shall any man be compelled to attend, erect or support any place of worship, or to maintain any ministry, against his consent; nor shall any control of, or interference with, the rights of conscience be permitted, or any preference be given by law to any religious establishments or modes of worship; nor shall any money be drawn from the treasury for the benefit of religious or theological seminaries.

Religious tests prohibited.

Section 19. No religious tests shall ever be required as a qualification for any office of public trust under the state, and no person shall be rendered incompetent to give evidence in any court of law or equity in consequence of his opinions on the subject of religion.

Section 23. Nothing in this constitution shall prohibit the legislature from providing for the safety and welfare of children by providing for the transportation for children to and from any parochial or private school or institution of learning.

Article X

EDUCATION

Section 3. The legislature shall provide by law for the establishment of district schools, which shall be as nearly uniform as practicable; and such schools shall be free and without charge for tuition to all children between the ages of four and twenty years; and no sectarian instruction shall be allowed there; but the legislature by law may, for the purpose of religious instruction outside the district schools, authorize the release of students during regular schools hours.

Wyoming

Article I

DECLARATION OF RIGHTS

Section 18. Religious Liberty. The free exercise and enjoyment of religious profession and worship without discrimination or preference shall be forever guaranteed in this state, and no person shall be rendered incompetent to hold any office of trust or profit, or to serve as a witness or juror, because of his opinion on any matter of religious belief whatever; but the liberty of conscience hereby secured shall not be so construed as to excuse acts of licentiousness or justify practices inconsistent with the peace or safety of the state.

Section 19. Appropriations for religion prohibited. No money of the state shall ever be given or appropriated to any sectarian or religious society or institution.

Article III

Section 36. Prohibited appropriations. No appropriation shall be made for charitable, industrial, educational or benevolent purposes to any person, corporation or community not under the absolute control of the state, nor to any denominational or sectarian institution or association.

Article VII

EDUCATION

Section 8. . . . nor shall any portion of any public school fund ever be used to support or assist any private school, or any school, academy, seminary, college or other institution of learning controlled by any church or sectarian organization or religious denomination whatever.

Section 12. Sectarianism prohibited. No sectarian instruction, qualifications or tests shall be imparted, exacted, applied or in any manner tolerated in the schools of any grade or character controlled by the state, nor shall attendance be required at any religious service therein, nor shall any sectarian tenets or doctrines be taught or favored in any public school or institution that may be established under this constitution.

Puerto Rico, Commonwealth of [6]

Article II

BILL OF RIGHTS

Section 1. The dignity of the human being is inviolable. All men are equal before the law. No discrimination shall be made on account of race, color, sex, birth, social origin or condition, or political or religious ideas. . . .

Section 3. No law shall be made respecting an establishment of religion or prohibiting the free exercise thereof. There shall be complete separation of church and state.

Section 5. . . . There shall be a system of free and wholly non-sectarian public education. Instruction in the elementary and secondary schools shall be free and shall be compulsory in the elementary schools to the extent permitted by the facilities of the state. No public property or public fund shall be used for the

---

6. Although Puerto Rico is not a state, it is possible that it will become one. The Commonwealth's constitution was adopted by a convention, ratified by the voters, and approved by the U.S. Congress in 1952.

support of schools or educational institutions other than those of the state.[7]

---

7. Congress in 1952 required as a condition of approval of the constitution that Puerto Rico amend Article II, Section 5 by adding the following language: "Compulsory attendance at elementary public schools to the extent permitted by the facilities of the state as herein provided shall not be construed as applicable to those who receive elementary education in schools established under non-governmental auspices."

Appendix I

Religious Freedoms Guaranteed by State Constitutions

State	Guaranteed Freedom of Worship or Conscience	No Establishment	No Required Church Attendance	No Aid to Sectarian Institutions	No Aid to Sectarian Schools	No Religious Test for Public Office	No Religious Test for Juries
Alabama	x	x	x		x	x	
Alaska		x		x	x		
Arizona	x			x	x	x	
Arkansas	x	x	x	x	x	x	x
Calif.	x	x		x	x		x
Colo.	x	x	x	x	x	x	
Conn.	x	x	x	x			

State	Guaranteed Freedom of Worship or Conscience	No Establishment	No Required Church Attendance	No Aid to Sectarian Institutions	No Aid to Sectarian Schools	No Religious Test for Public Office	No Religious Test for Juries
Del.	x	x	x	x		x	
Florida	x	x		x			x
Georgia	x			x		x	
Hawaii		x		x	x		
Idaho	x	x	x	x	x	x	
Illinois	x	x	x	x	x	x	
Indiana	x	x	x	x		x	x
Iowa		x	x	x		x	x
Kansas	x	x	x	x		x	x
Ky.	x	x	x	x	x		
La.	x	x		x	x	x	
Maine	x	x				x	
Md.	x		x	x		x	
Mass.	x			x	x		
Mich.	x		x	x	x	x	
Minn.	x	x	x	x	x	x	
Miss.	x				x	x	
Missouri	x	x	x	x	x	x	

State	Guaranteed Freedom of Worship or Conscience	No Establishment	No Required Church Attendance	No Aid to Sectarian Institutions	No Aid to Sectarian Schools	No Religious Test for Public Office	No Religious Test for Juries
Montana	x	x	x	x	x		
Nebr.	x	x	x	x	x	x	x
Nevada	x			x			x
N.H.	x	x			x		
N.J.	x	x	x	x		x	
N.M.	x	x	x	x			
N.Y.	x	x			x		x
N.C.	x						
N.Dak.	x	x					x
Ohio	x	x	x	x		x	x
Okla.	x			x		x	
Oregon	x			x		x	x
Pa.	x	x	x	x			
R.I.	x		x	x		x	
S.C.		x		x	x		
S.Dak.	x	x	x	x		x	
Tenn.	x	x	x	x		x	
Texas	x	x	x	x		x	x

State	Guaranteed Freedom of Worship or Conscience	No Establishment	No Required Church Attendance	No Aid to Sectarian Institutions	No Aid to Sectarian Schools	No Religious Test for Public Office	No Religious Test for Juries
Utah	x	x		x	x	x	x
Vermont	x		x	x			
Virginia	x	x	x	x	x		
Wash.	x			x	x	x	x
W.Va.	x		x	x			
Wis.	x	x	x	x	x	x	x
Wyo.	x			x		x	x
No. of States	46	35	29	42	25	31	18

Appendix II

Date of Admission to the Union

State	Date	Order	State	Date	Order
Alabama	Dec. 14, 1819	22	Idaho	July 3, 1890	43
Alaska	Jan. 3, 1959	49	Illinois	Dec. 3, 1818	21
Arizona	Feb. 14, 1912	48	Indiana	Dec. 11, 1816	19
Arkansas	June 15, 1836	25	Iowa	Dec. 28, 1846	29
California	Sept. 9, 1850	31	Kansas	Jan. 29, 1861	34
Colorado	Aug. 1, 1876	38	Kentucky	June 1, 1792	15
Connecticut	Jan. 9, 1788	5	Louisiana	Apr. 30, 1812	18
Delaware	Dec. 7, 1787	1	Maine	Mar. 15, 1820	23
Florida	Mar. 3, 1845	27	Maryland	Apr. 28, 1788	7
Georgia	Jan. 2, 1788	4	Massachusetts	Feb. 6, 1788	6
Hawaii	Aug. 21, 1959	50	Michigan	Jan. 26, 1837	26

State	Date	Order	State	Date	Order
Minnesota	May 11, 1858	32	Oregon	Feb. 14, 1859	33
Mississippi	Dec. 10, 1817	20	Pennsylvania	Dec. 12, 1787	2
Missouri	Aug. 10, 1821	24	Rhode Island	May 29, 1790	13
Montana	Nov. 8, 1889	41	South Carolina	May 23, 1788	8
Nebraska	Mar. 1, 1867	37	South Dakota	Nov. 2, 1889	40
Nevada	Oct. 31, 1864	36	Tennessee	June 1, 1796	16
New Hamp.	June 21, 1788	9	Texas	Dec. 29, 1845	28
New Jersey	Dec. 18, 1787	3	Utah	Jan. 4, 1896	45
New Mexico	Jan. 6, 1912	47	Vermont	Mar. 4, 1791	14
New York	July 26, 1788	11	Virginia	June 25, 1788	10
North Carolina	Nov. 21, 1789	12	Washington	Nov. 11, 1889	42
North Dakota	Nov. 2, 1889	39	West Virginia	June 20, 1863	35
Ohio	Mar. 1, 1803	17	Wisconsin	May 29, 1848	30
Oklahoma	Nov. 16, 1907	46	Wyoming	July 10, 1890	44

Suggestions for Further Reading

There are any number of good books on church-state relationships and the history of religious freedom in the United States. The following list includes some of the best that we have used repeatedly over the years.

Alley, Robert S., Jr. *The Supreme Court on Church and State.* New York: Oxford University Press, 1988. A thorough examination of the important rulings handed down by the nation's highest court and chief arbitrator of church-state disputes, with texts of the opinions.

————., ed. *James Madison on Religious Liberty.* Buffalo, N.Y.: Prometheus Books, 1985. A selection of Madison's key writings on religious liberty, plus 20 essays by distinguished scholars.

Blau, Joseph L. *Cornerstones of Religious Freedom in America.* Boston: Beacon Press, 1949. Brief historical sketches of the development of religious freedom in this country.

Brant, Irving. *The Bill of Rights: Its Origin and Meaning.* Indianapolis: Bobbs-Merrill, 1965. Authoritative history of the Bill of Rights. Contains a useful section on the development of the Fourteenth Amendment.

Butts, R. Freeman. *The American Tradition in Religion and Education.* Boston: Beacon Press, 1950. An overview of the role of religion in American education and a defense of religiously neutral public schools.

Butts, R. Freeman. *Public Education in the United States: From Revolution to Reform.* New York: Holt, Rinehart and Winston, 1978. History of American public education, including discussion of religious and church-state issues.

Cobb, Sanford H. *The Rise of Religious Liberty in America.* New York: Johnson Reprint Corporation, 1970. Though originally published in 1902, this remains one of the best historical surveys of how the constitutional principle of religious freedom was developed, nurtured and maintained on the soil of the U.S.A.

Cousins, Norman, ed. *In God We Trust.* New York: Harper and Row, 1958. An anthology of the major writings of nine seminal Founding Fathers, including Madison, Jefferson, Franklin, and Paine, and concentrating on their Enlightenment religious beliefs and ideas. Cousins' commentary is particularly illuminating. (This book was reissued in 1988 under the title *The Republic of Reason: The Personal Philosophies of the Founding Fathers.*)

Curry, Thomas J. *The First Freedoms: Church and State in America to the Passage of the First Amendment.* New York: Oxford University Press, 1986. An excellent history of the culture which produced the First Amendment.

Davis, Derek. *Original Intent: Chief Justice Rehnquist and the Course of American Church/State Relations.* Buffalo, N.Y.: Prometheus Books, 1992. A summary of constitutional jurisprudence relating to the First Amendment.

Doerr, Edd. *The Conspiracy That Failed.* Silver Spring, Md.: Americans United, 1968. A history of the dramatic 1967 campaign to amend New York's constitution to allow aid to parochial schools. Voters overwhelmingly rejected the proposal.

Doerr, Edd, and Albert J. Menendez. *Church Schools and Public Money: The Politics of Parochiaid.* Buffalo, N.Y.: Prometheus

Books, 1991. A history of the politics of parochiaid and the legal battles surrounding the issue at the federal and state levels.

Foote, Henry Wilder. *Thomas Jefferson: Champion of Religious Freedom.* Boston: Beacon Press, 1947. A slender but luminous interpretation of the role Jefferson played in the advancement of religious liberty in America.

Menendez, Albert J. *School Prayer and Other Religious Issues in American Public Education: A Bibliography.* New York: Garland Publishing, Inc. 1985. A guide to 1,566 books, articles, law review studies and dissertations, many of them relative to state constitutional questions.

———. *Church-State Relations: An Annotated Bibliography.* New York: Garland Publishing, Inc., 1976. A guide to 1,000 books in the field.

———. *Religious Conflict in America: A Bibliography.* New York: Garland Publishing, Inc. 1985. An annotated description of 1,410 books and articles relating to religious antagonisms and strife.

Menendez, Albert J., and Edd Doerr. *Religion and Public Education: Common Sense and the Law.* Long Beach: Centerline Press, 1991. A view of the major court rulings affecting the role of religious activities in public schools.

Miller, Robert T., and Ronald B. Flowers. *Toward Benevolent Neutrality: Church, State and the Supreme Court.* Waco, Tex.: Markham Press Fund of Baylor University Press, 1992. A monumental collection of all of the major U.S. Supreme Court decisions on church and state since 1872. An essential reference.

Must, Art, Jr., ed. *Why We Still Need Public Schools.* Buffalo, N.Y.: Prometheus Books, 1992. A collection of 23 illuminating essays on the importance of separation of church and state and of public education. Introduction by Connecticut Governor Lowell P. Weicker, Jr.

Peterson, Merrill D., and Robert C. Vaughn, eds. *The Virginia Statute for Religious Freedom.* New York: Cambridge University Press, 1988. A superior collection of essays probing the political culture which produced the Jeffersonian ideals of religious liberty and freedom of conscience for all citizens.

Pfeffer, Leo. *Church, State and Freedom.* Boston: Beacon Press, 1967. A thorough history of church-state relationships.

————. *God, Caesar and the Constitution.* Boston: Beacon Press, 1975. An examination of the role of the Supreme Court as referee between competing interests.

————. *Religion, State and the Burger Court.* Buffalo, N.Y.: Prometheus Books, 1984. A commentary on the increasingly frequent involvement of the Supreme Court as referee of church-state disputes during the 1970s and 1980s.

Stokes, Anson Phelps. *Church and State in the United States.* New York: Harper and Brothers, 1950. The definitive (three-volume) history of religious liberty and church-state relations in the U.S.

Stokes, Anson Phelps, and Leo Pfeffer. *Church and State in the United States.* New York: Harper and Brothers, 1964. A one-volume condensation of Anson Stokes' three-volume classic.

Swomley, John M. *Religious Liberty and the Secular State.* Buffalo, N.Y.: Prometheus Books, 1987. A summary of the foundations of religious freedom in America and an eloquent defense of the concept of secularity.

Wilson, John J., and Donald L. Drakeman. *Church and State in American History.* Boston: Beacon Press, 1987. A collection of primary source documents of inestimable value to students and researchers.

Wood, James. E., Jr. *Religion and the State: Essays in Honor of Leo Pfeffer.* Waco, Tex.: Baylor University Press, 1985. An admirable festschrift in honor of the dean of American constitutional lawyers.

Wood, James. E., Jr., ed. *Religion, the State and Education.* Waco, Tex.: Baylor University Press, 1984. An anthology of essays focussing on the complexities of religious activity in public education.